WORLD MYTHOLOGY

ODYSSEUS

B. A. Hoena

Consultant:
Dr. Laurel Bowman
Department of Greek and Roman Studies
University of Victoria
Victoria, British Columbia

Capstone
press

Mankato, Minnesota

Capstone Press
151 Good Counsel Drive, P.O. Box 669, Mankato, Minnesota 56002
http://www.capstonepress.com

Library of Congress Cataloging-in-Publication Data
Hoena, B. A.
    Odysseus / by B. A. Hoena.
    p. cm. — (World mythology)
    Summary: An introduction to the character of Odysseus and his importance in
Greek mythology.
    Includes bibliographical references and index.
    ISBN 0-7368-2498-7 (hardcover)
    1. Odysseus (Greek mythology)—Juvenile literature. [1. Odysseus (Greek mythology)
2. Mythology, Greek.] I. Title. II. Series: World mythology (Mankato, Minn.)
BL820.O3H64 2004
398.2′0938′01—dc22   2003012975

Editorial Credits

Juliette Peters, series designer; Patrick Dentinger, book designer and illustrator;
    Alta Schaffer, photo researcher; Eric Kudalis, product planning editor

Photo Credits

Art Resource/Scala, 14; Erich Lessing, 16, 20
Bridgeman Art Library/Hamburg Kunsthalle, Hamburg, Germany, 8; Musée des Beaux-Arts,
    Blois, France, 10; The Fine Art Society, London, UK/Private Collection, 18
Corbis/Araldo de Luca, cover (statue); Stapleton Collection, 4; Alexander Burkatowski, 12
Stock Montage, cover (ship), 1, 6

TABLE OF CONTENTS

Odysseus 5

Greek and Roman Mythical Figures 6

Homer 7

Odysseus' Wisdom 9

The Trojan War 11

Odysseus and Polyphemus 13

Odysseus' Adventures 15

Odysseus Returns Home 17

Penelope 19

Mythology Today 21

Places in Myth 22

Glossary 23

Read More 23

Useful Addresses 24

Internet Sites 24

Index 24

Odysseus stands toward the front of his ship in *The Ship of Odysseus with Oars and a Furled Sail* by Francois-Louis Schmied. Odysseus sailed the seas for many years before he could return home.

ODYSSEUS

One day, the Greek hero Odysseus (oh-DISS-ee-uhss) was visited by Prince Palamedes (pal-uh-MEE-deez) and Prince Menelaus (men-uh-LAY-uhss). They needed Odysseus' help. They were gathering an army to attack the city of Troy.

Odysseus did not want to help Palamedes and Menelaus. He wanted to stay home with his wife, Penelope, and his young son, Telemachus (tuh-LEM-uh-kuhss). So, Odysseus pretended to be insane. He hooked a donkey and an ox to his plow. He planted salt in his fields.

Palamedes thought Odysseus was only acting insane. He set Telemachus in front of Odysseus' plow. Palamedes knew that Odysseus would not run over his son if he was not insane.

Odysseus stopped the plow. Then, Palamedes and Menelaus knew that Odysseus was not insane. Odysseus had to go with them to fight the Trojans. Odysseus would be gone a long time and have many adventures before he could return home.

GREEK and ROMAN *Mythical Figures*

Greek Name: **ATHENA**
Roman Name: **MINERVA**
Goddess of wisdom and protector of heroes

Greek Name: **HELEN**
Roman Name: **HELEN**
Menelaus' wife

Greek Name: **HERMES**
Roman Name: **MERCURY**
Messenger of the gods

Greek Name: **MENELAUS**
Roman Name: **MENELAUS**
Greek prince married to Helen

Greek Name: **ODYSSEUS**
Roman Name: **ULYSSES**
Greek hero from Ithaca

Greek Name: **PENELOPE**
Roman Name: **PENELOPE**
Odysseus' wife

Greek Name: **PARIS**
Roman Name: **PARIS**
Trojan prince who took Helen from Menelaus

Greek Name: **POLYPHEMUS**
Roman Name: **POLYPHEMUS**
Cyclops who is Poseidon's son

Greek Name: **POSEIDON**
Roman Name: **NEPTUNE**
God of the sea

Greek Name: **ZEUS**
Roman Name: **JUPITER**
Ruler of the sky and the gods

HOMER

The Greek poet Homer lived about 800 B.C. He told of Odysseus' adventures in two long poems. Homer probably did not write down his poems. Few people knew how to read and write at the time. Instead, people listened to storytellers speak or sing poems aloud.

Homer's poem *The Iliad* tells about the Greek war against the city of Troy. This war is known as the Trojan War. Many people believe *The Iliad* is based on a real event. Historians believe the Trojan War was fought about 1250 B.C.

It took Odysseus 10 years to sail home after the Trojan War. Homer's poem *The Odyssey* tells about the adventures Odysseus had on his journey home.

Homer's stories about Odysseus are called quest myths. In quest myths, heroes performed very difficult tasks. Quest myths encouraged people. These stories taught people to never give up even if a task seemed impossible.

In the painting *Helen of Troy,* Dante Gabriel Rossetti shows how he imagined Helen may have looked. Greek and Roman myths say that Helen was the most beautiful woman in the world.

ODYSSEUS' WISDOM

Odysseus' parents were King Laertes (lay-UR-teez) and Queen Anticleia (an-ti-KLEE-uh). They ruled the island of Ithaca. Odysseus grew up to be a skilled hunter and a brave warrior. People also respected him for his wisdom. Odysseus showed his wisdom by helping King Tyndareus (tin-DER-ee-uhss) of Sparta.

Tyndareus had a very beautiful daughter named Helen. Odysseus and many other Greek princes wanted to marry her. But Tyndareus worried about the man Helen would marry. He was afraid the other men would kill Helen's husband out of jealousy.

Odysseus solved Tyndareus' problem. Odysseus said the men should take an oath before Helen picked a husband. They had to agree to protect the man Helen married. All of the men made this promise. Helen then picked Prince Menelaus to be her husband. Because they took an oath, none of the men harmed Menelaus.

Tyndareus rewarded Odysseus for his wisdom. He helped Odysseus marry Penelope. Penelope was Helen's cousin.

In *The Siege of Troy,* the Trojan horse stands inside the city of Troy.
Greek soldiers used the large, hollow horse to sneak into the city.

THE TROJAN WAR

The Trojan War began when Prince Paris of Troy took Helen from Menelaus. Menelaus led a Greek army to Troy to get his wife back. Odysseus and the men who had wanted to marry Helen joined Menelaus. They had promised to protect Helen's husband.

Myths say that gods built the walls around the city of Troy. The walls were too tall for the Greeks to climb over. They also were too strong for the Greeks to knock down. For 10 years, the Greek army failed to get inside and capture Troy.

Finally, Odysseus had an idea. He had a giant, hollow wooden horse built. The Greeks left the horse in front of the city gates. Then, the Greek army hid from the Trojans.

The Trojans thought the Greeks had left. They also thought the horse was a gift from the gods. The Trojans rolled the horse into Troy. They did not know that Greek soldiers were hiding inside the horse. That night, the Greek soldiers sneaked out of the horse. They opened the city gates, and the Greek army captured Troy.

In *Odysseus* by Jacob Jordaens, Odysseus and his men escape from Polyphemus. The men hid under sheep so the blind Cyclops could not find them.

ODYSSEUS AND POLYPHEMUS

Odysseus stopped on the island of Sicily as he sailed home from Troy. He needed to find food for his crew. In myths, one-eyed giants called Cyclopes (sye-KLOH-peez) lived on Sicily.

Odysseus hoped to befriend the Cyclopes. He wanted to ask them for help, but the Cyclopes did not like people. The Cyclops (SYE-klahpss) Polyphemus (pahl-i-FEE-muhss) trapped Odysseus and his men in a cave. Polyphemus then ate several of the men.

To escape, Odysseus blinded Polyphemus with a sharpened log while the monster slept. Odysseus and his men then hid under Polyphemus' sheep as the blind Cyclops tried to find them. The men crawled out of the cave and then ran to their ship.

Polyphemus asked his father to punish Odysseus for blinding him. Polyphemus' father was Poseidon, god of the sea. Poseidon raised storms to sink Odysseus' ship. For 10 years, the storms kept Odysseus from sailing home.

IOANES STRATENSIS
FLANDRVS 1570

Hermes (center) gives Odysseus (left) magic plants to eat in *Ulysses (Odysseus) and Circe* by Giovanni Stradano. Circe (seated right) feeds Odysseus' men a magic potion. The potion turns the men into animals.

Odysseus had many adventures as he tried to sail home. He met the witch Circe (SER-see). She turned some of his men into animals. The god Hermes gave Odysseus magic plants to eat. The plants stopped Circe from turning Odysseus into an animal.

Odysseus' men plugged their ears with beeswax when they sailed near the Sirens' island. The Sirens were birdlike women. They sang a beautiful song that made sailors forget what they were doing. The sailors' ships would crash on the island's rocky shore. Some myths say the Sirens then ate the drowning sailors.

Odysseus also sailed through the Strait of Messina. This waterway separates Sicily from Italy. There, Odysseus and his men met Charybdis (kuh-RIB-diss) and Scylla (SIL-uh). Charybdis was a whirlpool monster that sucked ships down to the bottom of the sea. Scylla was a six-headed monster living on a cliff along the Strait of Messina. As Odysseus' ship sailed by, Scylla snatched up one sailor in each of her six mouths.

Athena (center) is surrounded by Odysseus (right of Athena) and several other Greek heroes on this ancient Greek vase.

ODYSSEUS RETURNS HOME

Ancient Greeks and Romans believed that gods controlled their lives. In *The Odyssey*, the god Poseidon stopped Odysseus from sailing home to Ithaca. After 10 years, another god helped Odysseus return home.

The goddess Athena felt sorry for Odysseus. She asked Zeus, the ruler of the gods, to help Odysseus. Zeus agreed that Odysseus had suffered long enough. Zeus said Odysseus should be allowed to return home.

When Odysseus reached Ithaca, Athena warned him about the trouble he would find there. The rich young men of Ithaca were living in Odysseus' home. They wanted to marry his wife, Penelope, and had tried to kill his son, Telemachus. Athena said they would kill Odysseus if they found him.

Odysseus dressed as a beggar. Then, he went to his home. The men let him in when he begged for some food. Neither the men nor Penelope recognized Odysseus in his disguise.

In John Roddam
Spencer-Stanhope's
painting *Penelope*,
Penelope sits in front
of the death shroud
she was weaving for
King Laertes.

PENELOPE

Penelope suffered while Odysseus was away. She missed her husband. The rich young men of Ithaca tried convincing her that Odysseus was dead. They stayed in her home and would not leave. They also said she had to marry one of them.

Penelope said she would get married only after she finished weaving a death shroud for Odysseus' father, King Laertes. But Penelope tricked the men. During the day, she worked weaving. At night, she undid what she had worked on during the day.

Finally, Penelope had no choice. She had to marry one of the men before they destroyed her house. So, she said she would marry the man who could shoot Odysseus' large hunting bow. Each man tried, but none of them was strong enough.

Odysseus, dressed as a beggar, asked to shoot the bow. At first, the men laughed at him. But when he pulled the bowstring back, they knew he was Odysseus. Odysseus then used the bow to kill the men who had threatened his family while he was away.

In *Scylla and Charybdis* by Alessandro Allori, Scylla snatches up several men as Odysseus' ship sails past.

MYTHOLOGY TODAY

Long ago, people thought myths were true. Storytellers told myths about the Trojan War to teach history. People believed heroes like Odysseus were real people.

Today, people no longer believe in Greek and Roman myths, but names and words from myths are common. The planets in our solar system are named after Roman gods. Anyone who goes on a long trip is said to go on an "odyssey."

Myths also influence artists. Artists have created sculptures and paintings to show scenes from myths. Their artwork can be seen in museums. Authors have written books about stories from myths. *Ulysses*, by Irish author James Joyce, is a book based on Odysseus' adventures.

Myths are more than just exciting stories. They help people understand ancient cultures. Myths tell what people believed and show how people lived long ago.

PLACES IN MYTH

Rome

Adriatic Sea

ITALY

N
W • E
S

GREECE

•Troy

Aegean Sea

ITHACA

Thebes

Ionian Sea

Athens

SICILY   Strait of Messina

Sparta

KEY

• City

▲ Mount Olympus

SCALE
Miles

0   100   200

0   100   200
Kilometers

CRETE

Mediterranean Sea

GLOSSARY

ancient (AYN-shunt)—very old

beggar (BEG-ur)—a poor person who asks other people for food, money, and shelter

culture (KUHL-chur)—a people's way of life, ideas, art, customs, and traditions

Cyclopes (sye-KLOH-peez)—giants with one eye in the middle of their foreheads

disguise (diss-GIZE)—a costume that hides who a person is; Odysseus disguised himself as a beggar so people would not recognize him.

oath (OHTH)—a serious promise

quest (KWEST)—a journey taken by a hero to perform a task

shroud (SHROUD)—a cloth used to wrap a dead body

Trojan (TROH-jan)—a person from the ancient city of Troy, or having to do with the city of Troy, such as the Trojan War

wisdom (WIZ-duhm)—knowledge and good judgement

READ MORE

Green, Jen. *Myths of Ancient Greece.* Mythic World. Austin, Texas: Raintree Steck-Vaughn, 2001.

Hoena, B. A. *Athena.* World Mythology. Mankato, Minn.: Capstone Press, 2003.

USEFUL ADDRESSES

National Junior Classical League
422 Wells Mill Drive
Miami University
Oxford, OH 45056

Ontario Classical Association
P.O. Box 19505
55 Bloor Street West
Toronto, ON M4W 1A5
Canada

INTERNET SITES

FactHound offers a safe, fun way to find Internet sites related to this book. All of the sites on FactHound have been researched by our staff.

Here's how:
1. Visit *www.facthound.com*
2. Type in this special code **0736824987** for age-appropriate sites. Or, enter a search word related to this book for a more general search.
3. Click on the **Fetch It** button.

FactHound will fetch the best sites for you!

INDEX

Athena, 6, 16, 17
Circe, 14, 15
Helen, 6, 8, 9, 11
Homer, 7
Menelaus, 5, 6, 9, 11
Penelope, 5, 6, 9, 17, 18, 19
Polyphemus, 6, 12, 13
Poseidon, 6, 13, 17
Scylla, 15, 20
Trojan War, 5, 7, 10, 11, 21